SEAN DICKENS

Guatemala Travel Guide - Rio Dulce

Unveiling the Natural Wonders and Cultural richness of Guatemala

First edition

This book was professionally typeset on Reedsy.
Find out more at reedsy.com

Contents

1

Introduction

In northern Central America, just south of Mexico, lies a country that captures the essence of natural beauty and cultural richness like no other. Guatemala, with its lush tropical jungles, vibrant landscapes, indigenous heritage, and warm-hearted people, beckons travelers from around the world to uncover its hidden treasures. This travel guide will serve as an aid and companion for those embarking on a journey to experience the enchantment of Guatemala, with a particular focus on the breathtaking region of Rio Dulce.

LIBERTAD
15 DE
SEPTIEMBRE
DE 1821

It is my intention to provide travelers with an immersive and informative exploration of Rio Dulce, a mesmerizing destination nestled amidst the lush tropical rainforest and pristine waters of Guatemala. Through practical advice, and a dive into the region's history, culture, and attractions, my goal is for you to be equipped with the knowledge and inspiration necessary to make the most of your visit to this stunning corner of the world.

I hope to inspire a sense of wonder and adventure, encouraging you to step outside your comfort zone and embrace the diverse experiences that Rio Dulce has to offer. Whether you are a nature lover seeking solace in the wilderness, an avid explorer yearning to uncover ancient ruins, or a cultural enthusiast eager to engage with the local communities, this guide will help shape an unforgettable journey.

Nestled in the central eastern part of Guatemala, Rio Dulce presents a tapestry of natural wonders and cultural gems that leave visitors awe-struck. At the heart of this region is the eponymous Rio Dulce River, a majestic river snaking its way through dense jungles, towering cliffs, and tranquil lagoons. As you navigate the river's gentle currents, surrounded by vibrant foliage and exotic wildlife, you will soon realize why Rio Dulce has earned its reputation as a paradise for nature enthusiasts.

The area boasts a diverse array of attractions and highlights, each offering a unique glimpse into the wonders of Guatemala. Among the notable destinations is the stunning Lake Izabal, the largest lake in Guatemala. Its calm waters are perfect for a leisurely boat ride or a thrilling launcha adventure, the local mode of water transportation, allowing visitors to witness the lush shoreline and appreciate the tranquility of the surroundings.

For those with a penchant for history and archaeology, the nearby Mayan ruins of Tikal present an extraordinary opportunity to delve into the ancient civilization that once thrived in this region. The towering pyramids, and remnants of nearly 5,000 pre-hispanic buildings provide a glimpse into the rich cultural heritage of the Mayan people.

As you begin your journey up the Rio Dulce River, you will encounter the captivating town of Livingston, known for its Afro-Caribbean influence and vibrant Garifuna culture. Explore the narrow streets adorned with colorful houses, indulge in traditional cuisine, and immerse yourself in the lively rhythms of Garifuna music.

To truly appreciate the natural wonders of Rio Dulce, a visit to the Rio Dulce National Park is a must. This protected area encompasses dense rainforests, teeming with a variety of wildlife, including howler monkeys, jaguars, and a myriad of bird and insect species. Take a hike through the park's well-maintained trails, witness the cascading waterfalls, and let the symphony of nature envelop your senses. Whether you choose to embark on a river cruise, explore the vibrant culture, or lose yourself in the breathtaking landscapes, Rio Dulce promises an unforgettable adventure for every traveler.

This introduction sets the stage for a captivating exploration of Rio Dulce, Guatemala's crown jewel. As we embark on this journey together, prepare to be enthralled by the natural beauty, cultural richness, and warm hospitality that awaits you in this remarkable region. Through the pages of this book, we will navigate the rivers, traverse the jungles, and immerse ourselves in the wonders that make Rio Dulce an extraordinary destination. So, fasten your seatbelts, open your minds, and get ready to embark on an unforgettable adventure through the beauty of Guatemala's Rio Dulce.

2

Getting to Know Rio Dulce

Rio Dulce is a captivating destination on the eastern edge of Guatemala that attracts tourists from around the world. Here you will find a detailed overview of Rio Dulce, encompassing its geography, climate, natural landscape, and ecosystem. Additionally, it delves into the statistics of tourism growth, highlighting the region's popularity among travelers.

Recently, Rio Dulce has experienced a significant increase in tourism, establishing itself as a must-visit destination in Central America. The region's stunning natural beauty, coupled with its rich cultural heritage, has contributed to its popularity among travelers. According to recent statistics, tourism in Rio Dulce has witnessed a growth rate of approximately 10% per year, with an average of 300,000 visitors annually. The surge in tourism has had a positive impact on the local economy, creating employment opportunities and fostering sustainable development.

Rio Dulce is nestled in the central eastern part of Guatemala, serving as a link between Lake Izabal and the Caribbean Sea. The region is characterized by its picturesque river, also named Rio Dulce River, which meanders through lush rainforests and rugged cliffs. The river is flanked by towering limestone canyons, offering a breathtaking backdrop to the surrounding landscapes. Its strategic location makes Rio Dulce a gateway to exploring the diverse ecosystems of the surrounding area.

Rio Dulce experiences a tropical rainforest climate, characterized by high temperatures and abundant rainfall throughout the year. The average temperature ranges between 24°C (75°F) and 32°C (90°F), providing warm and humid conditions for visitors. The region receives the majority of its rainfall during the wet season, characterized by frequent rain showers and occasional thunderstorms, which typically extends from May to October. The dry season, on the other hand, spans from November to April, when rainfall is relatively lower and temperatures are slightly cooler.

Rio Dulce boasts a mesmerizing natural landscape that captivates visitors with its biodiversity and scenic beauty. The region is adorned with dense rainforests, cascading waterfalls, and serene lagoons, creating an enchanting environment for nature enthusiasts. The ecosystem of Rio Dulce is a haven for a diverse range of flora and fauna, making it a paradise for wildlife enthusiasts and bird watchers alike.

The rich biodiversity of Rio Dulce is evident through its lush tropical jungles. The rainforests surrounding the region are home to a plethora of plant species, including towering ceiba trees, colorful orchids, and vibrant heliconias. Wildlife enthusiasts can spot an array of animals, such as howler monkeys, toucans, parrots, jaguars, crocodiles and the ever elusive Quetzal, Guatemala's national bird.

The best time to visit Rio Dulce ultimately depends on personal preferences and interests. If witnessing the region's stunning waterfalls and vibrant flora is a priority, the wet season can be a rewarding experience. On the other hand, the dry season offers clearer skies and comfortable temperatures for exploring the region's natural wonders. It's worth noting that some activities, such as river cruises and water sports, are available year-round, providing visitors with a multitude of options regardless of the season.

Each season in Rio Dulce brings its own highlights and unique experiences. During the wet season, the region's waterfalls are at their most majestic, with increased water flow creating spectacular cascades. It is also an excellent time for bird watching, as many species are more active during this period. In contrast, the dry season provides opportunities for hiking and exploring the rainforests without the hindrance of heavy rainfall.

Overall, Rio Dulce's geographic beauty, diverse flora and fauna, and pleasant climate make it a captivating destination for nature lovers and adventure seekers alike. The region's growth in tourism reflects its increasing popularity, and visitors can expect a memorable experience immersed in the natural wonders of Rio Dulce.

3

Cultural Heritage - The Mayan Legacy

Rio Dulce is a region brimming with rich cultural heritage, primarily influenced by the ancient Mayan civilization. While in Rio Dulce you will have the opportunity to explore the Mayan history and influence in Guatemala. See the ancient Mayan ruins and archaeological sites that still captivate visitors today, as well as the customs and traditions of indigenous communities. Vibrant cultural events, rituals, and delicious cuisine make Rio Dulce a fascinating cultural destination that you will not soon forget.

The Mayan civilization, one of the most advanced pre-Columbian cultures in the Americas, flourished in what is now modern-day Guatemala. Rio Dulce served as an important waterway and trade route for the Mayans, connecting the highlands to the Caribbean Sea. The Mayans left a profound impact on the region's culture, architecture, art, and religious beliefs. Rio Dulce is home to several remarkable ancient Mayan ruins and archaeological sites, which offer glimpses into the civilization's intricate past. Notable sites include Quirigua, a UNESCO World Heritage site known for its intricately carved stelae. These intricate stelae are of immense archaeological importance. They offer insights into Mayan history, dynasties, and rituals depicting detailed portraits of rulers and providing crucial information about the hierarchies and relationships between different Mayan city-states.

Another significant, much larger site, is Tikal. Located a few hours from Rio Dulce, Tikal was once a powerful Mayan city covering nearly 16 square kilometers. Tikal was one of the largest Mayan cities in Central America and played a vital role in Mayan political and religious affairs. Rising far above the rainforest canopy, Tikal boasts impressive temples, palaces, and pyramids. These towering pyramids, such as Temple I and Temple II, symbolize the Mayan connection between Earth and the celestial realms. The ruins at Tikal highlight the city's grandeur, complex urban planning, and cultural significance. Exploring these sites provides visitors with an opportunity to marvel at the Mayan architectural prowess and gain insight into their religious and social practices.

Rio Dulce is home to various indigenous communities, such as the Q'eqchi' and Garifuna peoples, who have preserved their customs and traditions throughout the centuries. These communities maintain a strong connection to the land, practicing sustainable agriculture and engaging in traditional crafts. The Q'eqchi' people are known for their intricate weaving and vibrant textiles, while the Garifuna community showcases their unique music, dance, and drumming traditions. Engaging with these indigenous communities provides visitors with a chance to learn about their ancestral customs, language, and way of life.

Rio Dulce celebrates various traditional rituals and festivals throughout the year. One notable event is the Garifuna Settlement Day. Garifuna Settlement Day, a historical celebration in November, commemorates the arrival of West African Garifuna people in Central America. Their arrival, in the 19th-century, on the shores of Belize, Guatemala, Honduras and Nicaragua, is celebrated each year by vibrant, cultural holiday festivities, providing the Garifuna people occasion to honor their unique culture and ancestry.

Each year, week-long celebrations occur in towns up and down the coast, particularly in Dangriga, Punta Gorda, and Livingston, Guatemala, where lively parades, dramatic reenactments, joyful pageants, and sultry dancing in the streets attract thousands of local people waving flags and flowers, wearing traditional attire, singing and chanting to traditional Garifuna drumming and the reenactment of historical events. The region hosts cultural events that showcase the diversity of Mayan and Garifuna traditions. Rio Dulce offers a delectable array of traditional Mayan, Garifuna, and Latin cuisine. Dishes such as Jocon, Pepián, and Tapado showcase the region's unique blend of flavors and ingredients. Visitors can savor fresh seafood, tropical fruits, corn-based dishes, and aromatic spices, providing a gastronomic experience that reflects the region's cultural heritage.

Rio Dulce, Guatemala, stands as a testament to the lasting influence of the Mayan civilization. From the ancient ruins that speak of a bygone era to the vibrant customs, rituals, and festivals celebrated by indigenous communities, the cultural heritage of Rio Dulce is a treasure trove waiting to be explored. By engaging with the region's history, customs, and cuisine, visitors can gain a deeper understanding of the Mayan legacy and experience the living tapestry of traditions that make Rio Dulce a captivating cultural destination.

4

Outdoor Adventures and Natural Wonders

Whether you're interested in discovering local wildlife, exploring the river by boat, uncovering lesser-known attractions nearby, or relaxing in natural hot springs, Rio Dulce offers a plethora of activities for visitors to enjoy. We are going to explore the various activities and attractions that make Rio Dulce a destination you simply don't want to pass by.

Taking a tour by local boat or launcha is one of the best ways to experience the beauty of the Rio Dulce River. These tours provide a unique perspective of the river's lush surroundings, towering cliffs, and tranquil waters. You can hire a local guide who will navigate through the narrow channels and take you to hidden gems along the river. It's an excellent opportunity to soak in the breathtaking scenery and learn about the local culture and history.

When exploring the Rio Dulce River, there are several routes and locations you will not want to miss. One popular route is starting from the town of Fronteras and heading towards the Caribbean coast. Along the way, you'll encounter stunning landmarks such as the Castillo de

San Felipe de Lara, a historic fortress guarding the river's entrance. The fortress was built by the Spanish to protect against English pirates that sailed throughout the Caribbean. One of the most important tourist locations in the country, it functioned as a prison and military center. You can also visit Livingston, a vibrant Garifuna community, founded in the early 1800s and still known today for its Afro-Caribbean culture and Arawakan language.

Another prime spot not to be missed is Finca El Paraiso. Located about 30 minutes from Rio Dulce, by bus, near the town of Fronteras. Finca El Paraiso is a geo-thermal waterfall cascading into the cool river where you can take a rejuvenating swim in the heated waters. The Seven Altars waterfalls, near Livingston, also offer a refreshing way to cool off on a hot day. An easy 5 km hike from the beach brings you through the lush jungle to these seven cascading waterfalls. While it is a beautiful place year round, the best time to go is during the rainy season when the river and waterfalls are flowing at their peak capacities.

The Rio Dulce River basin is teeming with diverse wildlife, making it a haven for nature enthusiasts. Along the riverbanks and in the surrounding jungle, you can observe diverse bird species, including herons, kingfishers, hummingbirds, finches, ducks, parrots, and toucans, many species of frogs and toads as well as a plentiful number of butterflies. While traveling along the river make sure to keep an eye out for reptiles like crocodiles and iguanas sunning themselves on the river's edge. In addition to the hot springs, there are geothermal pools available in some resorts along the Rio Dulce. These pools are heated by underground volcanic activity and offer a tranquil setting to relax and rejuvenate. You can indulge in a soothing soak while enjoying panoramic views of the river and it's lush vegetation. Many resorts also offer spa services and therapeutic treatments, allowing you to further enhance your relaxation experience.

The Rio Dulce River and its surroundings offer a diverse range of activities and attractions. Whether you're seeking relaxation, wildlife encounters, historical exploration, or cultural immersion, this beautiful region of Guatemala has it all. Take your time to explore the river, uncover hidden gems, and create unforgettable memories along the way.

5

Culinary Experiences

Rio Dulce is not only renowned for its stunning natural beauty but also for its rich culinary traditions. Most foods in Central America have a similar latin or Spanish flair, however, the food in Guatemala is as diverse as the people that live here. Just like exploring the many different outdoor attractions and natural wonders, exploring local markets and savoring delicious street food is an adventure all its own. Rio Dulce has so many must-try dishes and hidden gems that will take you on a gastronomic journey through this enchanting region. Additionally, you will explore traditional recipes, highlight dining options, and discover establishments that offer exceptional flavors to make your culinary adventure in Rio Dulce truly unforgettable.

The diverse cultural heritage and culinary traditions of Rio Dulce are deeply rooted in the region. There are influences from the indigenous Mayan people, Afro-Caribbean communities, and Spanish colonies that create a fusion of flavors and techniques that make the food here a truly unique experience.

As is common in most third world countries, local markets abound along the main street in town. As you walk along you find yourself immersed in the local culinary culture that has been the normal way of life here for hundreds of years. There are multiple open air markets in town which offer a wide variety of fresh produce, meats, spices, and local ingredients. You will find many locals making fresh corn tortillas, roasting chicken of hot charcoal and offering fresh baked breads and rolls. Street food is an integral part of Rio Dulce's cultural heritage. Look out for food carts and stands that line the streets, offering mouthwatering snacks and quick bites. Some popular street food options include tamales, empanadas, pupusas (stuffed tortillas), and chuchitos (Guatemalan-style tamales). Take the time to wander through the market stalls, interact with the friendly vendors, and taste some of the regional delicacies.

One of the best culinary experiences you will experience is trying the Garífuna cuisine. The Garífuna people, with their Afro-Caribbean heritage, have contributed amazing and unique flavors to the region. Look for dishes like Tapado, a traditional seafood soup, found in many places throughout Livingston. Tapado is made with a flavorful broth of coconut milk, bananas, vegetables and a medley of fresh seafood such as fish, shrimp, and crab. The dish is typically served with rice and accompanied by tortillas, allowing you to soak up all the delicious flavors. Another traditional favorite is Hudut, a savory fish stew served with mashed plantains, and Sere, a coconut-based soup with fish and spices.

If you are adventurous and wish to truly appreciate the heritage of Rio Dulce, you must try your hand at preparing some of these traditional recipes yourself. One such recipe is the Pollo en Jocón, a classic Guatemalan chicken stew. The dish is made with a flavorful green sauce, primarily consisting of tomatillos, cilantro, green peppers, and spices.

The chicken is cooked in an aromatic sauce until tender and served with rice and tortillas. And then for dessert, indulge in the traditional sweet treat known as Rellenitos. Rellenitos are mashed plantains stuffed with a sweetened black bean paste and deep-fried until golden. The result is a delightful combination of sweet and savory flavors that will leave you craving more.

For those lacking the time or are just a bit more timid, Rio Dulce offers a range of dining options to suit every palate and budget. From casual eateries to upscale restaurants, you'll find a variety of establishments that showcase the region's culinary delights.

One popular restaurant in Rio Dulce is El Tortugal, known for its waterfront location and delicious seafood dishes. Here, you can savor fresh catches of the day, prepared with local flavors and served with stunning views of the river. If you're in the mood for international cuisine, Sun Dog is a fantastic choice. This quaint little river front restaurant offers a delectable array of dishes, including wood-fired pizzas providing a delightful change of pace from the traditional Guatemalan fare. If a bit more upscale is more your style then you can try Dreamcatchers, with their locally grown organic ingredients and imported meats, is for you. Or perhaps you would simply prefer the "best burger in Rio Dulce" at The Shack.

6

Unwinding in Paradise: Accommodations and Hospitality

Whether you're traveling on a budget or seeking a luxurious resort experience, Rio Dulce offers a range of accommodation options to suit every taste and preference. What follows is by no means everything that is available, but you will quickly see there are various accommodation options available, including boutique hotels and eco-friendly resorts, distinctive properties and their amenities, budget-friendly guesthouses and hostels, as well as affordable yet comfortable accommodations.

Rio Dulce boasts a handful of boutique hotels and eco-friendly resorts that provide a blend of luxury and sustainability. These hotels are designed to offer guests a unique experience yet remain as environmentally conscious as possible.

Nestled amidst a backdrop of lush jungle rainforest, Tortugal Boutique River Lodge offers comfortable rooms with style and stunning views of the Rio Dulce River. The hotel features conservative amenities like fiber optic wifi internet in every room, clean filtered fresh water, and laundry service. Guests can also cool off after a jungle hike in the delightful swimming pool, and then enjoy an exquisite dinner at the restaurant.

Catamaran Hotel is an extraordinary example of the diversity so commonly found along the Rio Dulce River. Not only is Catamaran a resort, but a very efficient marina as well. They have multiple docks, capable of handling up to 50' sail yachts, power yachts and catamarans providing guests with an extraordinary experience on the Rio Dulce River. The resort offers 34 comfortable fully air conditioned cabins, a restaurant serving delicious local recipes, and various activities like swimming, tennis, fishing, kayaking, and wildlife watching. It's an ideal choice for nature lovers and those seeking a unique accommodation experience.

Probably the most unique location in the entire Rio Dulce basin is an amazing eco-hotel called Hacienda Tijax. Opened in 1990, Hacienda Tijax consists of a rustic lodge, multiple cabins, marina, and restaurant all situated on 400 acres of tropical rainforest. Guests can enjoy amenities such as a swimming pool, hiking trails through the jungle, howler monkeys, horseback riding and kayaking along the river. They also provide tours to Livingston and the nearby Quiriguá Mayan Ruins.

The budget minded traveler has some excellent options in Rio Dulce as well. Hotel Kangaroo situated on a hilltop overlooking the Rio Dulce River offers comfortable rooms with breathtaking views starting at only $13 US. The property features swimming right from the dock in the river, a bar and a restaurant serving freshly prepared Guatemalan and Mexican cuisine. Relax in a hammock enjoying the surrounding landscape while reading a book or take a ride to town in the hotels launcha.

Hotel Backpackers sits on the banks of the Rio Dulce River, just a stone's throw from the town center. They offer private rooms as well as shared rooms at budget-friendly prices. They have a nice restaurant and amazing staff who can assist with arranging tours and transportation. Hotel Backpackers is also a part of Casa Guatemala, which is a registered NGO providing care for up to 300 children at a time. They help provide education, healthcare, nutrition and farming for Guatemalan children to learn what is needed for agriculture skills.

Casa Perico is a hidden gem on the banks of the Rio Dulce River. They offer both shared and private rooms as well as a private bungalow with a private bath. This quaint little hotel seems to be hidden in a remote part of the jungle, however, it's a mere 5 minute boat ride to the docks in town. Their small restaurant offers delicious recipes from Switzerland. They offer kayaks and canoes or they can help arrange tours to local sites like Livingston, San Felipe Castle or the ruins of Quiriga.

For those looking for higher end accommodations, Mar Marine Yacht Club will not disappoint. Situated on the riverfront, Mar Marine Yacht Club offers rooms with river views, suites and private apartments with small kitchens. They are a full service marina and boatyard with the capability to haul, repair and store boats. They feature a full service restaurant serving local dishes, a bar, and a terrace. Guests can enjoy activities like fishing, boat tours, kayaking and jet skies.

Rio Dulce offers a diverse range of accommodation options catering to different budgets and preferences. Whether you're looking for a luxurious boutique hotel, an eco-friendly resort, a distinctive property with unique amenities, a budget-friendly guesthouse, or an affordable yet comfortable stay, there are plenty of choices available in this charming Guatemalan town. By selecting the accommodation option that suits your needs, you can enhance your overall experience and make the most of your visit to Rio Dulce.

7

Navigating Rio Dulce: Transportation and Logistics

Getting to Rio Dulce can be an exciting adventure, with various options available including land, air, and sea travel. We are going to look at the different methods of transportation available to reach Rio Dulce, including international and domestic flight connections, overland travel options, and navigating within Rio Dulce itself using boats, ferries, taxis, and other local transportation services.

It is not actually possible to reach Rio Dulce by air, as there is no airport. However, you can arrive at one of Guatemala's major international airports and then make a domestic connection to a smaller regional airport closer to Rio Dulce. The primary international airports in Guatemala are La Aurora International Airport (GUA) in Guatemala City and Mundo Maya International Airport (FRS) in Flores.

La Aurora International Airport (GUA) is the largest and busiest airport in Guatemala and the fourth busiest airport in Central America, serving 20 international airlines with 24 destinations. Mundo Maya International Airport (FRS), the second main airport in Guatemala, is located in Flores, near the famous archaeological site of Tikal. Currently only servicing 5 airlines, it is still one of the busiest airports in Central America.

The most common and much more adventurous journey to Rio Dulce is by bus. Overland travel is an excellent option as Guatemala has a well-connected road network, making it possible to reach Rio Dulce by bus or car. By road, the journey from Guatemala City to Rio Dulce can take as little as 4-5 hours or as much as 17-20 hours, depending on traffic and road conditions.

Several bus companies offer services between Guatemala City and Rio Dulce. Some popular bus companies include Litegua, Monja Blanca, Linea Dorada as well as many smaller private options known as collectivo's. The most comfortable and usually the fastest choice is taking the large commercial bus from Litegua. They offer large reclining seats, air conditioning and many have WiFi onboard. It is advisable to book your bus ticket in advance, especially during peak travel seasons. While the cost of the large bus is very affordable, the cheaper option would be by way of the smaller collectivo. These are smaller buses, usually like a van, that carry fewer people. They are usually very inexpensive, but can take much longer to reach your destination. The most expensive option is to hire a private car or taxi that will take you directly to your destination. This option is the fastest way to get to Rio Dulce, depending on traffic conditions, but will also cost substantially more as well.

Renting a car is a convenient way to explore Guatemala and reach Rio

Dulce at your own pace. Many major car rental companies operate in Guatemala City, including Avis, Budget, Hertz, and National. Before embarking on your journey, it's essential to familiarize yourself with the local traffic laws and regulations. Keep in mind that driving in Guatemala can be challenging due to varying road conditions and driving habits. Exercise caution, particularly in rural areas where the roads may be less maintained.

Once you arrive in Rio Dulce, you'll find that boats and ferries are the primary means of getting around. Rio Dulce is famous for its picturesque river and lake system, making boats and ferries an integral part of transportation within the region. The town is situated on the banks of the Rio Dulce River, which flows into Lake Izabal. Many of the hotels and accommodations in Rio Dulce are only accessible by boat so they offer boat transfers to transport guests to their destinations. Additionally, public water taxis are available for short trips across the river or to nearby attractions.

Ferries and water taxis are also popular options for exploring the region. For example, you can take a ferry from Rio Dulce to Livingston, a vibrant coastal town known for its Garifuna culture. These ferries usually operate on a regular schedule and offer a unique way to experience the stunning landscapes along the river.

Taxis are also available in Rio Dulce for short journeys within the town or to nearby areas. The local taxi is a somewhat different option than most people are accustomed to seeing. Tuk Tuk's are the common "taxi" in Rio Dulce. A tuk tuk is a small three wheeled vehicle that is part motorcycle and part van. The driver sits in the center front seat while the passengers sit in the back seat. There are no doors and the roof is usually a soft canvas tarp. While in Rio Dulce you will see tuk tuk's driving up and down the streets quite frequently, as they are very nimble and can move through traffic very well. It is highly recommended to negotiate the fare before starting your trip and ensure the driver agrees on a fixed price.

Getting to Rio Dulce, Guatemala, offers a variety of exciting transportation options. Whether you prefer to travel by air, road, or water, there are suitable choices to suit your preferences and travel style. By exploring the international and domestic flight connections, overland travel options, and navigating within Rio Dulce using boats, ferries, taxis, and other local transportation services, you can embark on a memorable journey to this breathtaking destination.

8

Souvenirs and Shopping Experiences

Rio Dulce is a region rich in indigenous heritage and traditional crafts. The amazing shopping scene in Rio Dulce is an adventure in itself. You can explore an array of authentic indigenous crafts and artisanal products from traditional skilled artisans to local markets and street vendors. Come discover the true essence of Rio Dulce's shopping experience.

Rio Dulce is known for its vibrant indigenous culture, and the local artisans play a vital role in preserving traditional crafts. One of the most remarkable aspects of shopping in Rio Dulce is the opportunity to witness skilled artisans creating unique pieces by hand. You can find artisans specializing in various crafts, including textile weaving, pottery, woodcarving, basketry, and jewelry making. These artisans have honed their skills over generations, and their craftsmanship reflects the rich cultural heritage of the region.

Exploring the local markets in Rio Dulce is a delightful way to immerse yourself in the bustling atmosphere and discover a wide range of indigenous crafts and artisanal products. The markets are often energetic and colorful, brimming with an assortment of textiles, pottery, woven goods, and other handicrafts. These markets provide an excellent opportunity to interact with local vendors and gain insights into the indigenous culture and traditions.

One of the notable markets in Guatemala is the Mercado de Artesanias, located in the heart of Guatemala City. This market is renowned for its variety of traditional crafts, including intricately woven textiles, hand-painted ceramics, vibrant tapestries, and unique jewelry. As you navigate through the market stalls, you can engage with the vendors, learn about the different techniques and materials used, and appreciate the skill and creativity behind each item.

You will also find numerous street vendors scattered throughout Rio Dulce. These vendors offer an eclectic mix of handmade crafts and souvenirs, including beaded jewelry, hammocks, hand-carved figurines, and traditional clothing. Shopping from street vendors not only provides an opportunity to support local artisans directly but also offers a chance to find unique and one-of-a-kind pieces.

When shopping in Rio Dulce, authenticity is a key factor. The markets and artisanal shops in the region are dedicated to preserving traditional crafts and promoting fair trade practices. Purchasing from these establishments can ensure that your souvenirs are authentic and sustainably sourced.

Many of the handicrafts found in Rio Dulce make for excellent souvenirs or gifts. For example, textiles woven with intricate patterns and vibrant colors represent the region's textile traditions and can be transformed into clothing, wall hangings, or decorative items. Hand-painted ceramics showcase the craftsmanship of local potters, with designs inspired by the flora, fauna, and cultural symbols of the region. Additionally, intricately woven baskets, made from natural fibers, serve as functional and aesthetically pleasing pieces that reflect the indigenous traditions of Rio Dulce.

When selecting souvenirs, it is essential to consider the materials used and the craftsmanship involved. Opt for products made from sustainable materials and support artisans who use traditional techniques, ensuring the preservation of cultural heritage. By doing so, you not only bring home a piece of Rio Dulce but also contribute to the economic well-being of the local communities.

Shopping in Rio Dulce for indigenous crafts and artisanal products is a fascinating experience that allows you to delve into the region's rich cultural heritage. The skilled artisans and their traditional crafts, the lively local markets, and the abundance of authentic souvenirs make Rio Dulce a haven for those seeking meaningful and unique shopping experiences. By exploring the markets, engaging with artisans, and making conscious purchases, you can support the preservation of indigenous crafts and contribute to the local economy, all while taking home cherished mementos of your time in Rio Dulce.

9

Safety and Responsible Travel

Rio Dulce is a beautiful destination, however, like any travel destination, it is important to prioritize safety to ensure a pleasant and safe experience. We will discuss safety guidelines for visiting a third world country, general safety tips for travelers, health considerations and vaccinations, as well as responsible travel practices and ethical tourism.

Before your trip, it's a good idea to do some research and gather information about the area you are going to. Rio Dulce is not an unsafe place to visit, however, like most places in the world there are precautions you can take to make sure you have a pleasant and safe trip. Check travel advisories issued by your government and consult reliable sources to understand any potential risks or areas to avoid. Always choose reputable accommodations with good security measures and it's always a good idea to look for well-reviewed hotels or guesthouses that have positive feedback regarding safety. Consider factors such as well-lit premises, secure locks, and 24-hour reception or security. Use reputable transportation services for your journeys within Rio Dulce and when possible arrange transportation through your accommodation to minimize risks.

It is alway a good idea to keep your personal belongings secure at all times. Use a reliable lock for your luggage and find out if your hotel has secure locations such as a lockable safe to store valuables. When out in public, avoid displaying expensive jewelry or gadgets that may attract unwanted attention. When traveling outside the United States it is a good practice to carry a copy of your passport, identification, and other important documents while leaving the originals securely stored at your hotel. When traveling with cash, try to keep smaller amounts in your wallet so as not to attract unwanted attention. Avoid flashing large amounts of cash or valuable items, as this may make you a target for theft. Exercise caution when walking around unfamiliar areas, especially at night. Stick to well-lit and populated areas, and be aware of your surroundings. Save local emergency numbers on your phone and keep a printed copy of these numbers with you as well. It's important to have quick access to emergency services, medical assistance, and your embassy or consulate.

In some instances it can also be prudent to purchase comprehensive travel insurance that covers medical emergencies, trip cancellations, and personal belongings that may get stolen. Make sure to understand the terms and conditions of your policy before your trip. Stay updated with local news and developments and pay attention to any security alerts or changes in the local situation. Stay connected with your family or friends back home so if anything happens while you are traveling someone will know any changes in your itinerary. To avoid standing out as a tourist, dress modestly and try to blend in with the local culture. Respect local customs and traditions, which can contribute to a more positive and safer travel experience. While it's great to meet new people and make connections, exercise caution when interacting with strangers.

Avoid sharing personal or sensitive information with individuals you have just met, and trust your instincts if a situation feels uncomfortable.

Like most tropical countries there are always possibilities of contracting a disease or become sick from being bitten by insects. Guatemala, however, is a relatively safe country concerning these health concerns. Some people are worried about malaria, which can be an issue, but has not been a problem for many years. While quite rare, there have been a higher number of cases of dengue fever than that of malaria. Before traveling to Rio Dulce, consult a healthcare professional or a travel medicine specialist to discuss the necessary vaccinations and health precautions. Rio Dulce is located in a region where mosquito-borne diseases like dengue fever and Zika virus may be a concern. Use insect repellent, wear protective clothing, and consider staying in accommodations with screened windows or air conditioning.

As with most countries in Central America there is a much higher risk of waterborne illness if you drink tap water. It is highly advisable to drink bottled water or use water purification methods such as boiling or using water purification tablets. Be cautious with food hygiene, opting for freshly cooked meals and use good judgment when eating street food or raw/unpeeled fruits and vegetables.

Learn about the local customs, traditions, and etiquette in Rio Dulce. Respect the cultural practices and beliefs of the local communities, and be mindful of appropriate behavior in sacred or sensitive areas. Preserve the natural beauty of Rio Dulce by practicing responsible tourism. Respect protected areas, follow designated trails, and avoid littering. Support eco-friendly activities and tour operators that promote sustainability. Contribute to the local economy by supporting local businesses, purchasing authentic crafts and products, and engaging in community-based tourism initiatives. Respect the rights and livelihoods of local residents. Avoid activities that exploit or harm wildlife, such as supporting illegal animal trafficking or participating in activities that involve the mistreatment of animals. Choose responsible tour operators that prioritize animal welfare. Reduce your ecological footprint by conserving water and energy, properly disposing of waste, and using environmentally friendly products. Follow the principles of "leave no trace" and leave natural areas as you found them. By following these safety guidelines, practicing responsible travel, and respecting the local culture and environment, you can enjoy a secure and enriching experience while visiting Rio Dulce. Remember, your safety and the well-being of the destination's communities and natural resources go hand in hand.